Crash Course World History: A Study Guide of Worksheets for World History

By Roger Morante

Library of Congress Cataloging-in-Publication Date is available.

ISBN-13: 978-1-7322125-1-0
ISBN-10: 1732212511

Writer: Roger Morante
Cover Design: Artwork purchased from 99Designs.com.
Cover Artist: Amber_85
Editor: Roger Morante
Copy Editor: Erica Brown
Content Editor: John Te
Back Cover Photo: Liesl Morante
Publisher Logo: Isabella Morante

To contact the publisher send an email to the address below;
holden713@gmail.com

Additional copies may be purchased on Amazon.com or by contacting the author.

Printed in the United States of America

First printing June 2018

Table of Contents:

FORWARD

Dear students,

In writing Crash Course World History: A Study Guide of Worksheets for World History (2018) I confronted an issue that I did not have to confront in Crash Course US History: A Study Guide of Worksheets for US History (2018), and that is the usage of the date terms of BCE (Before Common Era) and CE (Common Era). I grew up in a world where BC referred specifically to the birth of Jesus Christ and stood for, "before Christ," while AD meant Addo Domini, Latin for, "in the year of the Lord." But as Pandora's box of knowledge opened before me and with it the free spread of information, I have come to understand why AD is not entirely inclusive of everybody and their respective religions on this earth. A brief study of the subject will reveal that the current usage of AD is entirely based upon the Gregorian Calendar with BC and AD initially set up by the Holy Roman Emperor Charlemagne in the 9th century and officially adopted by Western Europe in the 16th century. But in writing a book about world history I became concerned about the focus of world history as seen from an entirely Western European and Christian point of view. That said, this point of view has been extremely difficult to drive away from. Today we stand at these crossroads inside of the Age of Information where information flows freely. It is a system I hope remains in place in the future in order so that all may be able to judge a correct view of history determined by all the information available. That said I have concluded that the usage of BCE and CE is more inclusive of all rather than BC and AD. Yet I am also sensitive to those who do not want to give up the past usage of such a Gregorian system i.e. the usage of BC and AD. An argument could be made that If one did give up the Gregorian system, and say started counting using 4,000 BCE as a starting point, then the current year would be 6018 and we would be living not in the 21st century, but the 61st century. Somehow that realization seems foreign to me even though it may be argued as correct. I also do not think I am ready to change the date of my publication from 2018 to 6018. Also I know others still are entirely annoyed at the BCE and CE system but since common ground needs to be had, I propose a compromise system. For any of my crash course worksheets of where BCE and CE, or BC and AD, is in question, I will write the acronyms BCE and CE along with the date in order to clarify where in time the event occurred. But if the time period is not specified, i.e. BCE or CE, it should be assumed that I am dropping dates inside of the Common Era (CE) or if it is more palatable Addo Domini (AD) using the corresponding years in question. For example, dates in this book are written as such: **World War I** (1914-1919) instead of **World War 1** (1914-1919 CE). But when explaining the **Han Dynasty**, such as in the question, "Clarify the philosophy and position of the **Han** (202 BCE- 220 CE) **emperors** which began under **Emperor Wen** (202-157 BCE)," acronyms such as BCE and CE will be used interchangeably inside of the sentence.

Please enjoy the usage of this book along with John Green's Crash Course World History videos on YouTube and don't forget to turn on the captions in those videos to aid in understanding of the course in whatever language you feel most comfortable.

Sincerely, Roger Morante

The Agricultural Revolution: Crash Course World History #1

1) Describe the **process** it takes to make a cheeseburger.

_____
_____
_____
_____
_____
_____

2) Chronicle how humans **foraged** and **hunted** in order to subsist 15,000 years ago.

_____
_____
_____
_____
_____

3) Identify and analyze the origins of some **produce** and **crops.**

_____
_____
_____
_____
_____

4) Point out the advantages and disadvantages of switching from a **hunting-gathering society** to an **agriculture-based society.**

_____
_____
_____
_____
_____

5) Rationalize how the **production** of **grains** make **cities** possible.

_____
_____
_____

6) Compare and contrast the advantages and disadvantages of **farming**.

_____
_____
_____
_____

7) Outline the pros and cons of a life of **herding** in relation to a life of **foraging** and **agriculture**.

_____
_____

8) Give some examples of **domesticated animals** and what humans do with them.
   A)_____
   B)_____
   C)_____

9) Explain the theory of how **population pressure** necessitated the **agricultural revolution**.

_____
_____
_____
_____
_____
_____

10) Point out why YOU think the **agricultural revolution** was necessary for the advancement of the human race.

_____
_____
_____
_____
_____
_____

11) Name and explain some of the bad things that come with the introduction of **complex civilizations**.

_____
_____
_____
_____
_____
_____

Indus Valley Civilization: Crash Course World History #2

1) Explain the origins of the word **barbarian**.

_____

_____

_____

2) Identify the four stages of **human social development** and **organization** that classifies a group of peoples as a **civilization**.

A) _____

_____

_____

B) _____

_____

_____

C) _____

_____

_____

D) _____

_____

_____

3) Why did many early **civilizations** begin around **river valleys**?

_____

_____

_____

_____

4) Go into detail about why the **Bronze Age Indus Valley Civilization** (3300-1300 BCE) flourished around 3,000 BCE.

_____

_____

_____

_____

_____

5) How were homes in the cities of **Harappa** and **Mohenjo Daro** (in modern day **Pakistan**) built?

_____

_____

_____

_____

_____

6) Identify how the orientation of cities such as **Harappa** and **Mohenjo Daro** allowed them to remain cool even when it was really hot.

_____

_____

_____
_____

7) Explain how official **seals** helped to facilitate the trading of items such as **cotton cloth** that were made in these early **Indus River Valley** civilizations.

_____
_____
_____
_____
_____

8) Why do historians think that **Indus River Valley** people were peaceful and not warlike?

_____
_____
_____
_____
_____

9) Point out three theories for the decline of the **Indus River Valley** civilization.

A) _____
_____
_____

B) _____
_____
_____

C) _____
_____
_____

10) How can thinking about what motivated the **Indus River Valley Civilization** to thrive help us to think about how we structure our own lives?

_____
_____
_____
_____
_____
_____
_____
_____
_____
_____

Mesopotamia: Crash Course World History #3

1) Demonstrate the form of **socialism** that **farmers** engaged in around 5,000 years ago.

_____
_____
_____
_____
_____

2) How does the **Sumerian Epic of Gilgamesh** (2100 BCE) and its defining characteristic of **ziggurats** define a **city-state**?

_____
_____
_____
_____
_____
_____

3) Identify a number of the problems with living along the **Tigris** and **Euphrates Rivers** in ancient **Mesopotamia**.

_____
_____
_____
_____
_____
_____
_____

4) Clarify why the well-being and success of the **social order** shifted from the **gods** to the people.

_____
_____
_____
_____
_____

5) Point out the origins of the early **Mesopotamian** writing system called **cuneiform**.

_____
_____
_____
_____

6) Translate what **reading** and **writing** meant to the advancement of the **social order** and then identify the ensuing **class systems**.

_____
_____
_____

_____
_____
_____
_____

7) Analyze how the ability to **write** adds to the understanding of **history**.

_____
_____
_____
_____
_____
_____
_____

8) Evaluate how **Mesopotamia** become the world's first **territorial kingdom**.

_____
_____
_____
_____
_____

9) Throw light upon the concept of **private enterprise** and its relation to **taxes**.

_____
_____
_____
_____
_____
_____
_____

10) Reveal how Hammurabi (1810-1750 BCE), an early **monarch** in **Mesopotamia**, ran his **kingdom** from 1792-1750 BCE.

_____
_____
_____
_____
_____
_____
_____
_____

11) Examine the causes and effects around the creation and implementation of **Hammurabi's Code of Law** (1754 BCE).

_____
_____
_____
_____

_____

12) Identify and analyze what **territorial kingdoms** relied upon to work and function.

_____

13) Point out and explain who the **Assyrians** were and where their **empire** was located.

_____

14) Describe a **meritocracy** and how it relates to the structure of the **Assyrian army**.

_____

15) Briefly explain how the **Assyrians**, and their city of **Nineveh**, came to an end in 612 BCE.

_____

Ancient Egypt: Crash Course World History #4

1) How did the **Nile River** shape the **civilization** and viewpoints of the ancient **Egyptian** peoples living along its shores from 3,000 BCE- 332 BCE? (*BCE stands for Before Common Era)

_____

_____

_____

_____

_____

_____

_____

_____

_____

2) Explain the difference between the ancient **Egyptian civilization** (3,000 BCE – 332 BCE) and other similar **river valley civilizations**.

_____

_____

_____

_____

_____

_____

_____

_____

_____

_____

_____

_____

_____

3) Describe how **basin irrigation** was more functional and easier in **Egypt** than the complicated labor-intensive **hydraulic engineering projects** of other **river valley civilizations**.

_____

_____

_____

_____

_____

_____

_____

_____

4) Outline the basic differences in **religion** between the **Egyptians** and the ancient **Sumerians**.

_____

_____

_____

5) Define what the **Old Kingdom** (2649 BCE – 2152 BCE) in **Egypt** represented.

6) Describe the importance of the **Egyptian** sun-god **Ra.**

7) How did **cats** play a role in the religion of the **Egyptians**?

8) Analyze how the **Egyptian god Amun-Ra**, along with the advancements of the **Middle Kingdom (**2030 BCE to 1650 BCE), changed the religious structure **Egypt**.

_____
_____
_____
_____
_____
_____

9) How did **Egyptian pharaohs Akhenaten** (1380-1334 BCE) and **Tutankhamen** (1341-1323 BCE) throw light upon **monotheism** in the **New Kingdom** (1550-1077 BCE) of **Egypt**?

_____
_____
_____
_____
_____
_____
_____
_____
_____
_____
_____
_____
_____

10) Rationalize how the **Egyptian pharaoh King Tut** (**Tutankhamen**) (1341-1323 BCE) became so famous throughout the world even though he died at such a young age.

_____
_____
_____
_____
_____
_____
_____
_____
_____
_____
_____
_____
_____
_____

The Persians & Greeks: Crash Course World History #5

1) Who was **Herodotus** (484-425 BCE) and what is he famous for? (*BCE stands for Before Common Era)

_____
_____
_____
_____
_____

2) Outline the **Persian Empire** of **Cyrus the Great** (600-530 BCE) and **Darius I** (550-486 BCE), how they were related, and what that meant for **Mesopotamia**.

_____
_____
_____
_____
_____
_____
_____

3) Assess the advantages and disadvantages of being a **subject** inside of the **Persian Empire**.

_____
_____
_____
_____
_____
_____
_____
_____

4) Analyze the reasons for the success of the **monotheistic religion** of **Zoroastrianism** by comparing it to another religion of the time.

_____
_____
_____
_____
_____
_____
_____
_____
_____
_____

5) Who were the **Greeks** and how does ancient **Greek culture** influence modern day society?

_____
_____

_____
_____
_____
_____
_____
_____
_____
_____

6) Identify the high point of **Greek culture** and why it is known as such.

_____
_____
_____
_____
_____
_____
_____
_____

7) Analyze what the advantages were for the **Greeks** living in **city-states**.

_____
_____
_____
_____
_____
_____
_____
_____
_____
_____
_____
_____

8) Establish the reasons for the **Battle of Marathon** in 490 BCE between the **Persians** and the **Ionian Greeks** that ultimately lead to the **Persian Wars** (490-480 BCE).

_____
_____
_____
_____
_____
_____
_____
_____

9) Analyze the words of **Pericles** (495-429 BCE) and how they relate to **democratic laws** today.

_____
_____
_____

_____
_____
_____
_____

10) Outline the reasons for the conflict between **Athens** and **Sparta** in the **Peloponnesian Wars** (431-404 BCE) written during this time by historian **Thucydides** (460-395 BCE) in his book the **History of the Peloponnesian Wars**.

_____
_____
_____
_____
_____
_____
_____
_____
_____

11) Explain **Athenian democracy** using examples of why life may not have been that great during this time period.

_____
_____
_____
_____
_____
_____
_____
_____
_____
_____
_____
_____
_____
_____
_____
_____
_____

Buddha and Ashoka: Crash Course World History #6

1) Explain what is historically significant about the early **Indian Hindu** text the <u>**Vedas**</u> which were written in series using **Sanskrit** between 1500-1000 BCE.

_____
_____
_____
_____
_____

2) Analyze the **divinity** found in **Hindu** texts surrounding the origins of the **caste system** in **India**. _(Identify how it is divided into four parts)._

_____
_____
_____
_____
_____
_____
_____
_____

3) Summarize the epic **Sanskrit** tale of the **Mahabharata**.

_____
_____
_____
_____
_____
_____
_____

4) Identify and analyze the **social reasons** of having rules for **understood behavior** when following your **dharma**, or path, inside of the **caste system**.

_____
_____
_____
_____
_____
_____
_____
_____
_____

5) Explain the concept of **reincarnation** found in the **Sanskrit** word **samsara**.

_____
_____
_____
_____

_____
_____
_____
_____

6) Analyze the transcendent concept of **moksha** and how it fits into the theory of **karma** inside of the **religion** of **Hinduism**.

_____
_____
_____
_____
_____
_____
_____
_____

7) Outline the story of **Siddhartha Gautama** (563-480 BCE) also known as the **Buddha**.

_____
_____
_____
_____
_____
_____
_____
_____
_____
_____
_____

8) Explain the concept of **peace of mind** and the release from the **state of suffering** found in **nirvana**.

_____
_____
_____
_____
_____
_____
_____
_____
_____
_____

9) Identify and elaborate on the **four noble truths** found in **Buddhism**.

_____
_____
_____
_____

10) Identify and analyze the ideas that make up the **religious philosophy** of **Buddhism.**

11) Explain why **Indian Emperor Ashoka** (304-232 BCE) gave up everything to became a **monk**.

12) Determine the religious importance behind the **Buddhist** buildings named **stupas**.

13) Identify and analyze the core **philosophy** of **Buddhism.**

2000 Years of Chinese History! The Mandate of Heaven and Confucius:
Crash Course World History #7

1) Evaluate how **China** could be considered the first **modern state**.

_____
_____
_____
_____
_____
_____

2) Point out what makes a **dynasty** a **dynasty**.

_____
_____
_____
_____
_____
_____

3) Identify and analyze the life of **Chinese Empress Wu Zetian** (624-705 CE) who ruled during the later **Tang** (618-907 CE) dynasty. (*CE stands for Common Era)

_____
_____
_____
_____
_____
_____
_____

4) Describe the **Zhou** created concept of the **Mandate of Heaven**.

_____
_____
_____
_____
_____
_____

5) Explain the concept of **divine intervention** by pointing out how that relates to **dynasties** adhering to the **Mandate of Heaven**.

_____
_____

_____
_____
_____
_____
_____

6) Why is the **Qin dynasty** (221-206 BCE) considered so important to **China's** history?
(*BCE stands for Before Common Era)

_____
_____
_____
_____
_____
_____
_____
_____
_____
_____
_____
_____

7) Clarify the philosophy and position of the **Han** (202 BCE- 220 CE) **emperors** which began under **Emperor Wen** (202-157 BCE).

_____
_____
_____
_____
_____
_____
_____
_____
_____
_____
_____

8) Who was **Confucius** (551-479 BCE) and why was he so important to **Chinese** history?

_____
_____
_____
_____
_____

9) Contemplate whether or not **Confucianism** can be classified as a **religion**.

_____
_____
_____
_____

_____
_____

10) Why is the most important relationship in **Confucianism** between father and son?

_____
_____
_____
_____
_____
_____

11) Explain the philosophical term of **Junzi** and how it outlines proper behavior.

_____
_____
_____
_____
_____
_____

12) Compare and contrast the concepts of **Ren** (righteousness) and **Li** (ritual).

_____
_____
_____
_____
_____
_____
_____
_____

13) How do scholars agree is the best way to classify a good **emperor** in **China**? *(Be sure to include an example.)*

_____
_____
_____
_____
_____
_____
_____
_____
_____

Alexander the Great and the Situation...the Great?: Crash Course World History #8

1) What can be inherently wrong about labeling somebody in history as great?

_____

_____

_____

_____

_____

_____

_____

2) Give a quick **biography** on the origins and life of **Alexander of Macedonia** (356-323 BCE) also known as **Alexander the Great**. (*BCE stands for Before Common Era)

_____

_____

_____

_____

_____

_____

_____

_____

_____

_____

_____

_____

3) Point out the new **technology** used by **Alexander the Great** (356-323 BCE) and his armies.

_____

_____

_____

_____

_____

_____

_____

_____

4) Point out **Alexander the Great's** (356-323 BCE) shortcomings as a general and as king of the **Greek** armies.

_____

_____

_____

_____

_____

_____

5) Outline what happened to **Alexander the Great's** (356-323 BCE) empire shortly after his death in 323 BCE.

_____

_____

_____

_____

6) Identify how **Alexander the Great's** (356-323 BCE) post-mortem legacy led to the creation of **monarchies** in the **Greco-Roman** world.

_____

7) Examine and analyze the social, political, and economic repercussions **Alexander the Great** (356-323 BCE) had on culture in the **Hellenistic** world.

_____

8) Outline how history views and judges **Alexander the Great** (356-323 BCE) even though no accounts of him were written while he was alive.

_____
_____
_____
_____
_____
_____
_____
_____
_____
_____

9) How are **France's Napoleon** (1769-1821 CE) and **Greece's Alexander the Great** (356-323 BCE) connected throughout time?

_____
_____
_____
_____
_____
_____
_____
_____
_____
_____

10) Justify why the **Roman General Pompey's** (106 BCE- 48 BCE) hero was **Greece's Alexander the Great** (356-323 BCE) and how **Pompey** followed his lead.

_____
_____
_____
_____
_____
_____
_____
_____
_____
_____
_____
_____
_____
_____

The Silk Road and Ancient Trade: Crash Course World History #9

1) Explain how the **Silk Road** didn't begin **trade** but radically expanded it.

_____
_____
_____
_____
_____
_____

2) Gage the success of the **Silk Road** by including how things functioned along its **trade routes**.

_____
_____
_____
_____
_____
_____
_____
_____

3) Identify how **China** came to **monopolize** the **silk trade**.

_____
_____
_____
_____
_____
_____
_____
_____

4) Rationalize the social, political, and economic reasons for the types of **goods traded** by people living in and around the **Mediterranean Sea**.

_____
_____
_____
_____
_____
_____
_____
_____
_____

5) Reveal the origins of the **Silk Road** focusing on when it really took off and became a huge **hub** for the **silk route trade**, especially in towns along the way.

_____
_____

_____
_____
_____
_____

6) Untangle the problem with the **popularity** of wearing **silk** among many **elites** in **Rome**.

_____
_____
_____

7) Rationalize how the **merchant class**, which grew along with the **Silk Road**, came to have a lot of **political clout** (influence) which only further exacerbated the **tension** concerning the trade of **silk**.

_____
_____
_____
_____

8) Identify how the **Silk Road** affected the **economy** of the entire world.

_____
_____
_____
_____

9) Show how the **Silk Road** reshaped **religion** and helped to spread **Buddhism**.

_____
_____
_____
_____
_____
_____
_____
_____

10) Describe how **disease,** which spread along the **Silk Road**, changed the world.

_____
_____
_____
_____
_____
_____

The Roman Empire. Or Republic. Or...Which Was It?: Crash Course World History #10

1) Analyze how the **Roman Republic** utilized a balanced **government** blend of **monarchy**, **aristocracy**, and **democracy** in order to ensure its survival.

_____

_____

_____

_____

2) Unravel the innerworkings of the **blended political system** found inside of the **Roman Republic**.

_____

_____

_____

_____

_____

3) Justify how **ancient Romans** viewed the role of the **dictator** inside of the **Roman Empire**.

_____

_____

_____

_____

_____

4) Outline the life of Gaius **Julius Caesar** (100-44 BCE) and reveal his rise to power inside of the **Roman Republic**. (*BCE stands for Before Common Era)

_____

_____

_____

_____

_____

5) Briefly explain the complex **relationship** between Gaius **Julius Caesar** (100-44 BCE), Marcus **Crassus** (115-53 BCE), and Pompeius Magnus "**Pompey**" (106-48 BCE).

_____

_____

_____

6) Briefly summarize how the story of **Cleopatra** (69-30 BCE) and **Ptolemy XIII** (62-47 BCE) of **Egypt** mix in with the story of Gaius **Julius Caesar** (100-44 BCE).

_____

_____

7) Explain how the **dictator** Gaius **Julius Caesar** (100-44 BCE) restructured **Rome**.

8) How did Gaius **Julius Caesar** (100-44 BCE) identify his successor before he died?

9) Show how Gaius **Julius Caesar** (100-44 BCE) in effect destroyed the **Roman Republic**.

10) Analyze the repercussions the defeat of **Carthaginian General Hannibal** (247-181 BCE) by **Scipio** Aemilianus (185-129 BCE) at the end of the **Punic Wars** (264-201 BCE) had on the **Roman Empire**.

11) Why is it ridiculous to say that **Rome** was a **Republic** until **Emperor Augustus** (63 BCE -14 CE) became Rome's first official **emperor**?

Christianity from Judaism to Constantine: Crash Course World History #11

1) Who were the **Jewish** people (**Hebrews**) and where did they come from?

_____
_____
_____
_____
_____

2) Explain **monotheism** and what it had to do with **Judaism**.

_____
_____
_____
_____
_____
_____

3) Draw conclusions as to how the idea of a **covenant** affected **Judaism**.

_____
_____
_____
_____
_____
_____

4) Asses the concept of **singularity** and how it applies to **Judaism**.

_____
_____
_____
_____
_____

5) Who were the **Romans** and what was their role in absorbing the **province** of **Judea**?

_____
_____
_____
_____
_____
_____
_____
_____

6) Analyze the life and death of **Jesus of Nazareth** (4 BCE- 33 CE). (*BCE stands for Before Common Era and *CE stands for Common Era)

_____
_____
_____
_____
_____
_____
_____
_____
_____
_____
_____

7) Why do YOU think so many people at the time thought that **Jesus** was the **Messiah**?

_____
_____
_____
_____
_____
_____

8) Why do YOU think that the above belief in **Jesus** as the **Messiah** became so widespread?

_____
_____
_____
_____
_____
_____

9) Briefly compare the similarities and differences between the **Roman Emperor Augustus** and **Jesus of Nazareth**.

_____
_____
_____
_____
_____
_____
_____

10) Explain what happened to the **Jewish** peoples during a revolt around 66-73 CE.

_____
_____
_____
_____

11) How did the **religion** of **Judaism** splinter to form **Christianity**?

_____

_____

_____

_____

_____

_____

_____

12) Who was **Saul of Tarsus** (5-67 CE), aka Paul the Apostle, and what role did he play in the spread of **Christianity**? (*aka means also known as)

_____

_____

_____

_____

_____

_____

_____

13) Why do YOU think **Christianity** flourished inside of the **Roman Empire**?

_____

_____

_____

_____

_____

_____

_____

_____

14) What role did the **Roman Emperor Constantine** (272-337 CE) play in the spread of **Christianity**?

_____

_____

_____

_____

_____

_____

_____

_____

_____

Fall of the Roman Empire...In the 15th Century: Crash Course World History #12

1) Outline the **classical view** for the **Fall** of the **Roman Empire**.

_____
_____
_____
_____
_____

2) Argue in support of **Roman senator** and historian **Tacitus'** (14-70 CE) theory that **Rome** was "doomed to fall" as soon as it spread outside of **Italy**. (*CE means Common Era)

_____
_____
_____
_____

3) How did the **Roman mantra, "to rule with an iron fist,"** ultimately lead to the decline of the **Roman Empire**?

_____
_____
_____
_____
_____

4) Rationalize why the incorporation of **German warriors** into the **Roman army** was a really bad decision on the part of the **Roman Empire** and ultimately led to **civil war**.

_____
_____
_____
_____
_____

5) Point out the reasons why the **Eastern Roman Empire** (aka the **Byzantium Empire**) survived until the **15th century**. (*aka means also known as)

_____
_____
_____
_____
_____

6) Why did **Emperor Constantine** (272-337 CE) move the capital of the **Roman Empire** to the **East** in 324 CE instead of keeping it in **Rome**?

_____
_____

7) Clarify why **Emperor Constantine** (272-337 CE) has been identified with **Christianity** and how he helped to spread **Christianity** throughout the **Roman Empire**.

8) Explain the continuity between the old **Western Roman Empire** and the new **Eastern Roman Empire**.

9) Analyze why the most consistently **Roman** aspect of **Byzantine society** included how they followed **Roman law**.

10) To what degree did **Roman Emperor Justinian** (482-565 CE), in the **Latin** law book **Digest** (aka **Justinian Law Code**) compiled in 530-533 CE, influence **Roman laws**?

11) What did **Empress Theodora** (500-548 CE) do to further the **rights of women** in the **Eastern Roman Empire**?

12) How did **Charlemagne's** (742-814 CE) crowning strain relations in the **Roman Empire** and ultimately lead to a split between the **Western Catholic** and **Eastern Orthodox churches**?

Islam and the Quran: Crash Course World History #13

1) Evaluate the origins of **Islam** around the time when the archangel **Gabriel** was believed to have appeared to the prophet **Muhammad** (570-632 CE).

_____

_____

2) Describe the type of society in which **Muhammad** (570-632 CE) lived.

_____

_____

_____

3) Point out the other religions besides **Islam** which were also around in **Arabia**.

_____

_____

_____

4) At its core, outline the tenants of the **religion** of **Islam**.

_____

_____

_____

_____

5) Identify the **main themes** prevailing throughout the **Quran**.

_____

_____

_____

_____

6) Describe the **first pillar** of **Islam**.

_____

_____

_____

7) Describe the **second pillar** of **Islam**.

_____

_____

_____

8) Describe the **third pillar** of **Islam**.

_____

_____

_____

_____

9) Describe the **fourth pillar** of **Islam**.

_____
_____
_____
_____

10) Describe is the **fifth pillar** of **Islam**.

_____
_____
_____
_____

11) Connect the **religious law** of **sharia** with **Islam**.

_____
_____
_____
_____

12) What is the significance about the city of **Medina**?

_____
_____
_____
_____

13) What happened in 630 CE in the city of **Mecca**?

_____
_____

14) Explain why the **caliph** split into the two major sects of **Islam**: the **Sunni** and the **Shi'a**. *Include the disagreement around who was to succeed the prophet **Muhammad** (570-632 CE) after his death.*

_____
_____
_____
_____

15) How large did the **Muslim** empire expand? *(Include as many countries as you can.)*

_____
_____

16) Evaluate the significance of the spread of **Islam** in the **Middle East**.

_____
_____
_____
_____

The Dark Ages...How Dark Were They, Really?: Crash Course World History #14

1) Why is the period between 600 and 1450 in **Europe** called the **Middle Ages**?

_____
_____
_____
_____
_____
_____

2) Briefly describe what **conditions** were like in the cities of **London, England** and **Paris, France** during the **Middle Ages** (600-1450).

_____
_____
_____
_____
_____
_____

3) Clarify the **health** situation inside of **Europe** during the **medieval times**.

_____
_____
_____
_____
_____
_____

4) Explain the **political system** of **feudalism** which dominated the **politics** of the **Middle Ages** (600-1450).

_____
_____
_____
_____
_____
_____
_____

5) Go into detail about how **feudalism** was also an **economic system**.

_____
_____
_____
_____
_____

6) Why wasn't a **feudalistic** type of **medieval world** conducive to **social mobility**?

_____
_____
_____
_____

7) How did **superstition** come to dominate **European** thought?

_____

_____

_____

_____

_____

8) Reveal how the **Umayyad Arabs** under their **religion** of **Dar Al-Islam** placed themselves at the top of the established **hierarchy.** *(Be sure to include what eventually led to their downfall in 750.)*

_____

_____

_____

_____

_____

9) Describe how the **Abbasids**, who ruled from 750-1258, took on a distinctly **Persian** cast.

_____

_____

_____

_____

_____

10) Illuminate how the openness of the **Abbasids** and their tolerance to foreigners was good for the proliferation of their **empire** with their new **capital** in **Baghdad**.

_____

_____

_____

_____

_____

_____

11) Describe how early **Islamic** science made huge strides in **medicine**.

_____

_____

_____

_____

_____

12) Interpret the thinking of **Andalusian philosopher Ibn Rushd**. (1126-1198).

_____

_____

_____

_____
_____
_____
_____
_____
_____
_____

13) Describe how the city of **Cordoba** in **Spain** become the center for the **arts** and **architecture**?

_____
_____
_____
_____
_____
_____
_____
_____

14) Explain how the rise of the **Tang Dynasty** (618-907) in **China**, also known as the **Golden Age of China**, ran parallel to the **Dark Ages** (476-1492) of **Europe**.

_____
_____
_____
_____
_____
_____
_____
_____

15) Briefly describe how the **Chinese** capitalized on **inventions** such as iron, paper money, porcelain, and gun powder during the **Dark Ages** (476-1492).

_____
_____
_____
_____
_____
_____
_____
_____
_____
_____
_____
_____

The Crusades : Crash Course World History #15

1) Explain how **faith** drove **military expeditions**, called the **Crusades** (1096-1291), from parts of **Europe** to the **Eastern** coast of the **Mediterranean**.

_____
_____
_____
_____
_____

2) How does **Pope Urban II's** (1035-1099) initiation of the **First Crusade** (1096-1099) play into the **Holy Land** shifting the focus to **Jerusalem**?

_____
_____
_____
_____
_____
_____
_____

3) Why were the **Crusades** (1095-1291) NOT an example of early **European colonization**?

_____
_____
_____
_____
_____
_____

4) Identify the **social status** of the **knights** who took part in the **Crusades** (1095-1291).

_____
_____
_____
_____
_____

5) From the point of view of the **Crusaders**, what were they doing in the **Holy Land**?

_____
_____
_____

6) How did the **Crusaders** reverse a seemingly hopeless situation during the **Siege of Antioch** (1097-1098) against the **Muslim**-held city?

_____

_____
_____
_____
_____
_____
_____
_____

7) Explain the importance of **Sultan Saladin's** (1137-1193) taking of **Jerusalem** in the **Battle of Hattin** (1087) from the **Crusaders** with his **Muslim** forces.

_____
_____
_____
_____
_____
_____
_____
_____
_____

8) Explain why the capturing of the cities of **Acre** and **Jaffa,** located inside of modern day **Israel,** during the **Third Crusade** (1189-1192), led to it becoming the most famous **crusade**.

_____
_____
_____
_____
_____
_____
_____
_____
_____
_____

9) Explain why the **Fourth Crusade** (1202-1204) is considered the crazy **crusade**.

_____
_____
_____
_____
_____
_____
_____
_____
_____
_____

10) Identify the importance of **Byzantine Emperor Alexios III Angelos** (1153-1211) and clarify his promise made to the **crusaders**.

_____
_____

_____
_____
_____
_____
_____

11) Identify how the **Fourth Crusade** (1202-1204), legitimized crusading.

_____
_____
_____
_____
_____
_____
_____
_____
_____

12) Why didn't the **Crusades** (1095-1291) open up new **lines of communication** between the **Christians** and the **Muslims**?

_____
_____
_____
_____
_____
_____
_____
_____
_____

13) Explain why the **Crusades (**1095-1291) mattered in the **medieval** world.

_____
_____
_____
_____
_____
_____
_____
_____
_____
_____

Mansa Musa and Islam in Africa: Crash Course World History #16

1) Recount the legendary tale of the sultan **Mansa Musa** (1280-1337).

_____
_____
_____
_____
_____
_____
_____

2) Identify the importance surrounding the tale of **Mansa Musa** (1280-1337).

_____
_____
_____
_____
_____
_____
_____
_____

3) Explain what **Mansa Musa's** kingdom in **Mali, West Africa** looked like.

_____
_____
_____
_____
_____
_____
_____
_____
_____
_____

4) Who were the **Berbers** and how did the **Berbers** influence **Islam**?

_____
_____
_____
_____
_____
_____
_____
_____
_____

5) Identify and analyze the differences between the **monotheistic** religion of **Islam** and the traditional **polytheistic** religion inclusive of multiple **African gods**.

_____
_____
_____

_____
_____
_____
_____
_____
_____
_____
_____

6) Go into detail about the **Hajj** and why **Muslims** make this **pilgrimage** to **Mecca** annually.

_____
_____
_____
_____
_____
_____
_____
_____
_____
_____
_____
_____
_____
_____

7) Consider why **Ibn Battuta** (1304-1377) has been considered one of the most travelled **West Africans** of his day.

_____
_____
_____
_____
_____
_____
_____
_____
_____
_____
_____

8) Analyze the development of **Swahili** civilization in **Eastern Africa**.

_____
_____
_____
_____

_____
_____
_____
_____

9) Identify and reflect on the three items that constituted the culture of the **Swahili city states**.

_____
_____
_____
_____
_____
_____
_____
_____
_____
_____
_____

10) Identify the types of **goods** that were exported out of **East Africa** along the **Silk Road**.

_____
_____
_____
_____
_____
_____
_____
_____

11) How should **historians** and students of history study the history of **Africa**?

_____
_____
_____
_____
_____
_____
_____
_____
_____
_____
_____

Wait for it...The Mongols!: Crash Course World History #17

1) What are the three key things to remember when identifying a **herder**?
   A)_____

   _____

   B)_____

   _____

   C)_____

   _____

2) Explain why **pastoral** people tend to be **egalitarian**.

   _____

   _____

   _____

   _____

3) Outline the origins of the **Mongols**.

   _____

   _____

   _____

4) Identify the origins of **Genghis Kahn** (1162-1227) and how he came to lead the **Mongols** to dominate the world.

   _____

   _____

   _____

   _____

5) Outline how **Genghis Kahn's** (1162-1227) policies concerning **military structure** worked to win over the **peasant classes** he conquered.

   _____

   _____

   _____

   _____

6) Analyze how the **Mongols** chose their leaders.

   _____

   _____

   _____

7) Outline a few of the reasons for the success of **Genghis Khan's** (1162-1227) armies.

   _____

   _____

   _____

   _____

   _____

   _____

   _____

   _____

   _____

8) Explain the five reasons why the **Mongols** were so awesome.

A)_____

_____

_____

_____

B)_____

_____

_____

_____

C)_____

_____

_____

_____

D)_____

_____

_____

_____

E)_____

_____

_____

_____

9) Analyze five key reasons why the **Mongols** may not have been so great.

A)_____

_____

_____

_____

B)_____

_____

_____

C)_____

_____

_____

_____

D)_____

_____

_____

E)_____

_____

_____

_____

Int'l Commerce, Snorkeling Camels, and the Indian Ocean Trade:
Crash Course World History #18

1) Compare the **Indian Ocean trade** to trade along the **Silk Road**.

_____
_____
_____
_____
_____
_____

2) Identify the reasons why **Indian Ocean trade** took off and became a key factor in **East-West** exchanges.

_____
_____
_____
_____
_____
_____
_____
_____

3) Explain why **predictable winds** were so important to the **Indian Ocean trade**.

_____
_____
_____
_____
_____
_____

4) Show how **Indian Ocean trade** incorporated more people than the **Silk Road trade**.

_____
_____
_____
_____
_____

5) Why is studying the paths of **Muslim merchants** important in understanding **Indian Ocean trade** along the **Western** half of the **Indian Ocean**?

_____
_____

_____
_____
_____
_____

6) Illustrate the hardships faced by the **Kashmir's Hindu** queen **Kota Rani** up until her death in 1339.

_____
_____
_____
_____
_____
_____

7) Point out the good thing about **trade bulk goods** exchanged in the **sea trade**.

_____
_____
_____
_____
_____
_____

8) What did the continent of **Africa** produce that was traded in the **Monsoon Marketplace**?

_____
_____
_____
_____
_____
_____
_____

9) Identify the different types of **produce** that were traded inside of the **Monsoon Marketplace**.

_____
_____
_____
_____
_____
_____
_____

10) Clarify the importance of having and using the **navigational tool** of the **astrolabe**.

_____
_____
_____
_____

_____

_____

11) Identify the reasons why the **triangular lateen sail**, invented inside the **Muslim** world, became so important in the **Monsoon Marketplace**.

_____

_____

_____

_____

_____

_____

12) Rationalize the reasons why more **Muslims** lived in **Indonesia** than in any other country.

_____

_____

_____

_____

_____

_____

13) Show how a specific **region** could became the center of **trade**.

_____

_____

_____

_____

_____

_____

14) Analyze why YOU think the imposition of **taxes on traders** in the **Monsoon Marketplace** motivated **merchants** to find other **trade routes**.

_____

_____

_____

_____

_____

_____

Venice and the Ottoman Empire: Crash Course World History #19

1) By what means was the city of **Venice** constructed? *(Be sure to include how its geography lead to its growth relying on **trade**.)*

_____

_____

_____

_____

_____

_____

2) How did **Venice** establish itself as the biggest **European** power in the **Mediterranean**?

_____

_____

_____

_____

_____

_____

3) Explain how the body of **Christian Evangelist St. Mark,** who died in 68 CE, ended up in a church in the **Piazza San Marco** in **Venice, Italy**.

_____

_____

_____

_____

_____

_____

4) Reveal the **trade secrets** as to how the **Venetians** became famous for their **textiles** and **glass making**.

_____

_____

_____

_____

_____

_____

5) Briefly describe the **political system** of government found in the city of **Venice**.

_____

_____

_____

_____

_____

6) Briefly describe the **political system** of government found in the **Ottoman empire**.

_____

_____

_____
_____
_____
_____
_____

7) Describe how **Suleiman the Magnificent** (1494-1566), who ruled from 1520-1566, came to **dominate trade** during the **golden age** of the **Ottoman Empire** (1301-1922).

_____
_____
_____
_____
_____
_____
_____
_____
_____

8) Analyze why the **empire** that the **Ottomans** ruled was much more valuable than the **empire** the **Romans** ruled.

_____
_____
_____
_____
_____
_____
_____
_____
_____

9) Point out how the **Ottoman Empire** created an entirely new ruling class governed under a system called **slave aristocracy**.

_____
_____
_____
_____
_____
_____
_____
_____

Russia, the Kievan Rus, and the Mongols: Crash Course World History #20

1) Briefly analyze the origins of the **settlers** who came the Russian city of **Kiev**.

_____
_____
_____
_____

2) Describe how **agriculture** shaped one's **social status** and **tax burden** in **Kiev**.

_____
_____
_____
_____

3) How did **Russia** become a **Byzantine Christian** nation?

_____
_____
_____
_____

4) Define **appanage** and explain what was going on during the period known as **Appanage Russia** during the 11th to 14th centuries.

_____
_____
_____
_____

5) As rulers, elaborate how did the **Mongols** treated their **Russian subjects**.

_____
_____
_____
_____

6) Why does history view it as important that the **Russians** were cut off from the **Byzantine Empire** after the **Mongolian invasions**?

_____
_____
_____
_____
_____
_____

7) Explain how the **Mongols** were integral in the shaping of the **Russian** capital city of **Moscow**.

_____

_____

_____

_____

8) How did the physical location of **Moscow** help it to become well-positioned for **trade** throughout **Russia**?

_____

_____

_____

_____

9) Calculate how **Moscow** became the seat for the **Eastern Orthodox church** in 1325.

_____

_____

_____

_____

10) Why was the **Battle of Kulikovo** (1380) so important in the shaping of **Russian** history?

_____

_____

_____

_____

11) Who was **Ivan III** (1440-1505), aka **Ivan the Great,** and how did he establish **Moscow** as the center of an independent **Russian state**? (*aka means also known as)

_____

_____

_____

_____

12) Point out and evaluate the reasons why the Russian **autocratic** ruler **Tzar Ivan IV** (1530-1584) came to be known and remembered as **Ivan the Terrible**.

_____

_____

_____

_____

13) Briefly explain how, in the centuries following **Ivan the Terrible** (1530-1584), **Russia** was seen by the rest of **Europe** as **European** but also as not.

_____

_____

_____

_____

Columbus, de Gama, and Zheng He! 15th Century Mariners!:
Crash Course World History #21

1) Analyze the life and accomplishments of expeditionary voyager and **Chinese Admiral Zheng He** (1371-1435).

_____
_____
_____
_____

2) Briefly describe the types of ships used by **Zheng He's** (1371-1435) massive **armada** in both the **Indian** and **Pacific Oceans**.

_____
_____
_____

3) Describe what was going on in **China** when **Zheng He** (1371-1435) was sailing with his fleet in the **Indian** and **Pacific Oceans**.

_____
_____
_____
_____

4) Identify the social, political, and economic reasons why **Zheng He's** (1371-1435) **voyages** to the **Indian** and **Pacific Oceans** ended.

_____
_____
_____
_____

5) Outline the reasons why the **Great Wall of China** was built. (_Include the **dynasty** responsible for the feat._)

_____
_____
_____
_____

6) Assess the competitive advantages the **Portuguese** had in **exploration** under **Portuguese** navigator **Vasco de Gama** (1460-1524).

_____
_____
_____
_____

7) Describe the **cartaz** strategy that **Portuguese navigator Vasco de Gama** (1460-1524) used in order to expand the overseas **empire** of the country of **Portugal**.

_____
_____
_____
_____

8) Dispel some of the myths surrounding **Italian** navigator **Christopher Columbus** (1446-1506) who sailed in the name of **Spain**.

A) _____
_____
_____
_____

B) _____
_____
_____
_____

C) _____
_____

9) Analyze the reasons behind the **Line of Demarcation** (1494) and the repercussions of the dispute settled between **Portugal** and **Spain** during the **Age of Discovery** (15th-18th centuries) by **Pope Alexander VI** (1431-1503).

_____
_____
_____
_____

10) Describe the voyages of **Christopher Columbus** (1446-1506) and include how he convinced **Spanish King Ferdinand** and **Queen Isabella** to fund his voyages.

A) _____
_____
_____
_____
_____

B) _____
_____
_____
_____

C) _____
_____
_____
_____

The Renaissance: Was it a Thing? Crash Course World History #22

1) Examine what was so controversial about how the **Renaissance** (1300-1600) ushered in the modern era of **secularism**, **rationality**, and **individualism**.

_____

_____

_____

_____

_____

_____

2) What is meant by the term **classism** when referring to **Renaissance art**?

_____

_____

_____

_____

_____

3) Identify why **humanists** were advocates of **liberal arts** during the **Renaissance** period.

_____

_____

_____

_____

_____

_____

4) Explain the social, political, and economic factors which made the **Italian city states** ripe to usher in the birth of the **Renaissance** (1300-1600).

_____

_____

_____

_____

_____

_____

_____

_____

5) Gage how trade with the **Ottoman Empire** provided the **Italian city states** with all the money it needed to launch the **Renaissance** (1300-1600).

_____

_____

_____

_____

_____

_____

6) Why were **Florentine textiles** so valuable around the **Mediterranean Sea**?

_____

_____

_____

_____

_____

_____

7) How did the **Medici family** come to wield such massive control over **Florence** during the **15th and 16th centuries**?

_____

_____

_____

8) How did the **Fall of Constantinople in 1453** help to further spread **Greek ideas**?

_____

_____

_____

_____

_____

9) Analyze the reasons why most people in **Europe** were totally unaware that the **Renaissance** (1300-1600) was going on around them.

_____

_____

_____

_____

_____

_____

10) Rationalize the importance of the **Renaissance** (1300-1600) as being able to incorporate **Aristotle**'s views of **individualism** as seen in the art of **Michelangelo, Leonardo Da Vinci, Rafael,** and **Donatello**.

_____

_____

_____

_____

_____

_____

_____

_____

The Colombian Exchange: Crash Course World History #23

1) Identify the four categories of the **Columbian Exchange** and then explain each category in the questions that follow.   A) _____
B)_____ C) _____ D)_____

2) Calculate the initial response of the **Native Americans** to the arrival of the **Europeans**. *(Include the types of **diseases** spread by the **Columbian Exchange**.)*
_____
_____
_____
_____
_____

3) Analyze the **secondary effects** of the **European diseases** which spread throughout the **Americas**.
_____
_____
_____
_____

4) Explain how **Spanish conquistador Hernán Cortés** led an expedition that caused the fall of the **Aztec Empire**.
_____
_____
_____
_____
_____

5) Describe how the **venereal disease** of **syphilis** was spread throughout **Europe**.
_____
_____
_____
_____
_____

6) Justify the reasons why **European animals** were so revolutionary when introduced to the **Americas**.
_____
_____
_____
_____
_____
_____
_____
_____
_____

7) How have **domesticated animals** introduced from **Europe** changed the **landscape** of the **Americas** both in **food production** and **transportation**?

_____

_____

_____

_____

8) Explain how the introduction of **American plants** and **crops** to **Europe** radically changed the lives of hundreds of millions of people.

_____

_____

_____

_____

_____

_____

9) Why do you think the **world population doubled** between 1650 and 1850?

_____

_____

_____

_____

_____

10) Explain how the **Colombian Exchange** involved the **transfer** of people.

_____

_____

_____

_____

_____

_____

11) Explain the problems critics have surrounding the **Colombian Exchange**.

_____

_____

_____

_____

_____

_____

_____

_____

The Atlantic Slave Trade: Crash Course World History #24

1) Analyze the numbers and percentages involved in the European countries participating in the **slave trade** prior to the trading of **slaves** in the **Americas**.

_____
_____
_____
_____
_____
_____
_____
_____
_____
_____
_____
_____

2) Critique the **consumer culture** responsible for growing of the **primary crops** such as sugar, tobacco, and coffee by **slaves**.

_____
_____
_____
_____
_____
_____

3) How did **slave owners** see **slaves** as an **economic commodity** rather than as human beings?

_____
_____
_____
_____
_____
_____
_____
_____

4) Describe the conditions **slaves** endured when travelling to the new world on **slave ships**.

_____
_____
_____
_____
_____
_____
_____
_____
_____

5) Describe the **market** in which **slaves** were traded and sold once they arrived to the **United States**.

_____

_____

_____

_____

6) Point out and explain the brutality behind the **working conditions** of **slaves** both in the **United States** and in other parts of the **Americas**.

_____

_____

_____

_____

_____

_____

_____

_____

_____

_____

_____

_____

_____

_____

_____

_____

7) Explain the correct definition of the word, "**slave**."

_____

_____

_____

_____

8) What makes the institution of **slavery** so horrendous?

_____

_____

_____

_____

_____

9) Describe how the word **cattle** came from the old French word, **chattel**?

_____

_____

_____

_____

10) How did churchgoing Bible-worshipping **Christians** morally justify the institution of **slavery**?

_____
_____
_____
_____
_____
_____
_____
_____
_____
_____
_____

11) Analyze the truth that we must grapple with today over how our **ancestors** defined the **attitude** people in the **New World** had toward **slaves**.

_____
_____
_____
_____
_____
_____
_____
_____
_____
_____
_____
_____
_____
_____
_____
_____
_____
_____
_____
_____
_____
_____
_____
_____
_____

The Spanish Empire, Silver, & Runaway Inflation: Crash Course World History #25

1) Explain the origins of the **Mesoamerican** civilization known as the **Aztecs** (1300-1521) and include how their civilization functioned.

_____
_____
_____
_____
_____
_____

2) Outline the **territory** conquered by the **Aztecs** (1300-1521) by mapping out the extent of their **empire**.

_____
_____
_____
_____

3) Why was it easy for **Hernán Cortés** (1485-1547) to come into **Mexico** and find allies to overthrow the **Aztecs** (1300-1521)?

_____
_____
_____
_____
_____

4) Rationalize the strategic importance surrounding the construction of the **Aztec** capital of **Tenochtitlán**.

_____
_____
_____
_____
_____

5) Analyze the techniques rulers of the **Incan civilization** (1438-1533) used in order to **assimilate** conquered people into their **empire**.

_____
_____
_____
_____
_____
_____
_____
_____

6) Why do YOU think **disease** wiped out much of the **Incan civilization** (1438-1533) soon after the arrival of the **Spanish** in 1532?

_____
_____
_____
_____
_____

7) Explain why it was so easy for the **Spanish** to set up a new system of **government** in the **New World** to control the **Incans** and the **Aztecs**.

_____
_____
_____
_____
_____
_____
_____

8) Point out the lust **Spanish conquistadors** had for **Aztec** and **Incan gold** and then determine how successful or unsuccessful their attempts were to attain it.

_____
_____
_____
_____
_____
_____

9) Show how the **Spanish** borrowed and intensified the **Mit'a system** of the **Inca Empire** (1438-1533) in order to establish the **encomienda system**.

_____
_____
_____
_____
_____
_____
_____
_____

The Seven Years War: Crash Course World History #26

1) Explain what was going on in the global **Seven Years War** (1756-1763).

_____
_____
_____
_____
_____

2) Spell out how the **economics** of **trade** caused the **Seven Years War**(1756-1763) between the **British colonists** and the **French**.

_____
_____
_____
_____
_____

3) Interpret how the **French** came to the conclusion that **British-Atlantic trade** was making **Britain** rich and prosperous.

_____
_____
_____

4) Point out the role that future United States President **George Washington** (1732-1799) played in support of the **British** during the **Seven Years War (**1756-1763).

_____
_____
_____

5) Analyze how the death of **General James Wolfe** (1727-1759) at the **Battle of the Plains of Abraham** in 1759 was memorialized.

_____
_____
_____
_____

6) Describe what **Native American tribes** were doing as the **British** and **French** were fighting during the **Seven Years War** (1756-1763).

_____
_____
_____
_____
_____
_____

7) Investigate and report what **Native Americans** were doing in **North America** prior to the arrival of the **Europeans**.

_____

_____

_____

_____

8) Rationalize the ideas **Native Americans** had concerning **property** and how that was different then the **European** point of view.

_____

_____

_____

_____

_____

9) Identify and analyze what the **British** and the **French** were fighting over in the **Caribbean** islands.

_____

_____

_____

_____

10) Point out how **disease** played a large role in decimating both the **French** and **British** armies during the **Seven Years War** (1756-1763).

_____

_____

_____

_____

11) Identify the reasons why the **British** and **French** were fighting each other in the colonies of **Africa**.

_____

_____

_____

_____

12) Examine what happened during the **Black Hole of Calcutta** event on June 20, 1756 that occurred to prisoners during the **Seven Years War** (1756-1763).

_____

_____

_____

_____

13) Analyze both the **economic** and **human cost** of the **Seven Years War** (1756-1763) after the signing of the **Treaty of Paris of 1763** to end the war.

_____

_____

_____

_____

The Amazing Life and Strange Death of Captain Cook: Crash Course World History #27

1) Consider and reflect upon the impact of the **voyages** undertaken by **British** explorer, navigator, and cartographer **Captain James Cook** (1728-1779).

_____

_____

_____

_____

_____

_____

2) Briefly analyze the reasons why **Rudyard Kipling** wrote the poem "The White Man's Burden: The United States and the Philippine Islands," (1899) and show how this relates to the **American** philosophy of **Manifest Destiny**.

_____

_____

_____

_____

_____

_____

_____

_____

_____

3) Investigate and report on how **Captain Cook** (1728-1779) died in 1779 soon after the second time he landed in **Kealakekua Bay** off the Kona coast of the island of **Hawaii**.

_____

_____

_____

_____

_____

4) Examine and analyze a quick paraphrase of Marshall Sahlins book, **Islands of History** (1985), and link how **Captain Cook's** (1728-1779) death at the end of **Makahiki** fits perfectly with the ritual structure of **Hawaiian culture**.

_____

_____

_____

_____

_____

_____

_____

_____

5) Analyze the **opposing point of view** from Anthropology Professor Gananath Obeyesekere about **Captain Cook's** [1728-1779] death which strays from the popular view that **Captain Cook** was killed as part of a **Hawaiian ritual sacrifice**.

_____
_____
_____
_____
_____
_____
_____

6) Take into consideration the **fracas** which occurred during **Captain Cook's** [1728-1779] second visit to **Hawaii** and interpret the probable **truth** about how **Captain Cook** died.

_____
_____
_____
_____
_____
_____

7) Point out how there had been rising tensions between the **Hawaiians** and the **Europeans** prior to **Captain Cook's** [1728-1779] death in 1779.

_____
_____
_____
_____
_____
_____

8) Even with the evidence pointing towards **Hawaiians** not seeing **Captain Cook** [1728-1779] as a **god**, why do many historical interpretations still consider **Captain Cook's** death as a case of mistaken identity?

_____
_____
_____
_____
_____
_____
_____
_____
_____

Tea, Taxes, and The American Revolution: Crash Course World History #28

1) Explain the reasons why the **American colonists** reacted negatively to the **Stamp Act of 1765** imposed on them by the **British Parliament**.

_____

_____

_____

_____

_____

_____

2) How did the repeal of the **Stamp Act of 1765** only further embolden the **colonists** to **protest** against new **taxes** such as those found in the **Townshend Acts** of 1767 and 1768?

_____

_____

_____

_____

_____

_____

3) Point out and explain the social, political, and economic reasons that ultimately led to a street fight that came to be known as the **Boston Massacre of 1770.**

_____

_____

_____

_____

_____

_____

_____

_____

_____

_____

4) Rationalize the **irony** around what occurred during the **Boston Tea Party of 1773**.

_____

_____

_____

_____

_____

_____

5) How did the **Committees of Correspondence** effectively help the **colonists** protest the unfair **taxation without representation** levied by **the British Government**?

_____
_____
_____
_____
_____
_____
_____
_____

6) Outline what the **First Continental Congress of 1775** was most famous for doing.

_____
_____
_____
_____
_____

7) Show how the **Committees of Correspondence** worked in setting up the first self-governing **shadow governments** in the fledgling **United States**.

_____
_____
_____
_____
_____
_____

8) Outline and explain the main problems with the short-lived **United States government** supported by the **Articles of Confederation** (1783-1789).

_____
_____
_____
_____
_____
_____
_____
_____
_____
_____
_____
_____
_____

_____
_____

9) Briefly describe the main ideas swimming around in **colonial society** during the 18th century, aka the **Age of Reason** or the **Age of Enlightenment**. (*aka means also known as.)

_____
_____
_____
_____
_____
_____
_____
_____
_____
_____

10) Identify how **Americans** came to view themselves as **equal** to each other after the **American Revolution** (1775-1783).

_____
_____
_____
_____
_____
_____
_____
_____
_____
_____
_____
_____

11) Outline how the basic ideas surrounding the **American Revolution** (1775-1783) came to fruition.

_____
_____
_____
_____
_____
_____
_____
_____
_____
_____
_____

The French Revolution: Crash Course World History #29

1) Outline the structural problems **French society** faced during the 18th century.

_____
_____
_____
_____
_____
_____

2) Identify the repercussions of **French King Louis XVI** (1754-1791) futile attempts to solve the problem of **France's** ballooning **national debt** in the 18th century.

_____
_____
_____
_____
_____
_____

3) Point out how **Prussian Enlightenment** philosopher **Immanuel Kant** (1724-1804) challenged the idea of **religion**.

_____
_____
_____

4) Show how the **Estates General of 1789,** which reformed itself into a **National Assembly** with the **Tennis Court Oath of 1789,** marked the beginning of the **French Revolution** (1789-1799).

_____
_____
_____
_____
_____
_____
_____
_____

5) Outline what happened on **Bastille Day** (14th of July, 1789) and why it marked a turning point in the **French Revolution** (1789-1799).

_____
_____
_____

6) Interpret the fundamental rights that the **Declaration of Rights of Man and Citizen** of 1789 gave to all **French** male **citizens**.

_____
_____
_____
_____
_____

7) Show how the **Jacobins** (1792-1794) were the most influential **political club** during the **French Revolution** (1789-1799).

_____
_____
_____
_____

8) Evaluate the actions of monarchs **King Leopold of Austria** (1640-1705) and **King William Frederick II of Prussia** (1744-1797 CE) took with the issuing the **Declaration of Pillnitz of 1791** to restore the **French monarchy**. _(Include how that action backfired.)_

_____
_____
_____
_____
_____

9) Show how the death of **Louis XVI** led to **Committee of Public Safety** head **Maximilien Robespierre's Reign of Terror** in **France**.

_____
_____
_____
_____

10) Briefly outline how **Napoleon Bonaparte** (1769-1821) rose through the ranks of the **military** during the **French Revolution** (1789-1799) to ultimately become **emperor** of **France** from 1804-1815.

_____
_____
_____
_____

11) Why do YOU think the **French Revolution** (1789-1799) is so controversial and open to interpretation today?

_____
_____
_____
_____
_____
_____

Haitian Revolutions: Crash Course World History #30

1) Explain the **repercussions** felt on the **Caribbean** island of **Saint-Domingue**, modern day **Haiti**, after the **French** convinced the **buccaneers** to give up piracy in the late 17th and early 18th centuries.

_____
_____
_____
_____
_____

2) Analyze and reflect upon the working conditions of **African slaves** and connect it to the **class structure** of the **society** of those living on **Saint-Domingue** in the late 17th and early 18th centuries.

_____
_____
_____
_____
_____

3) How did the different members of the **Saint-Domingue society** react to the outbreak of the **French Revolution** (1789-1799) in **France**?

_____
_____
_____
_____
_____

4) Explain how the ideas inside the legal document, **The Declaration of Rights of Man** of 1789, influenced the ideas of liberty, fraternity, and equality, and also indirectly caused the **slave uprising** and subsequent **Haitian Revolution of 1791**.

_____
_____
_____
_____
_____
_____

5) Point out how the leadership of African-born slave **Toussaint L'Ouverture** earned the freedom of every French slave in the **Caribbean** during the **Haitian Revolution**.

_____
_____
_____
_____
_____

6) Identify the historical significance of the **Haitian Revolution** of 1791.

_____

_____

_____

_____

_____

7) Identify and evaluate the reasons for the second phase of the **Haitian Revolution** that began in 1802. *(Include **Napoleon Bonaparte's** role in sparking this revolution.)*

_____

_____

_____

_____

_____

_____

_____

_____

_____

8) How did the spread of **Yellow Fever** on the island of **Saint-Domingue** help the **Haitians** to win their **independence**?

_____

_____

_____

_____

9) Briefly outline the reasons why **Napoleon** sold the **Louisiana Purchase** to the **United States of America** in 1803.

_____

_____

_____

_____

_____

_____

10) Paraphrase the ideology found inside of the **Haitian Declaration of Independence** of 1804.

_____

_____

_____

_____

_____

_____

Latin American Revolutions: Crash Course World History #31

1) By what **methods** did **Spain** and to an extent **Portugal** exercise their **control** over the **native populations** in the **Americas**?

   a) The **Spanish Crown**:

   _____

   _____

   _____

   _____

   b) The **Catholic Church**:

   _____

   _____

   _____

   _____

   c) The **Patriarchy**:

   _____

   _____

   _____

   _____

2) Point out how the Spanish **patriarchy** influenced the life of **Sor Juana Inez de la Cruz** (1651-1695).

   _____

   _____

   _____

   _____

   _____

   _____

3) How did **cultural blending** in **Latin America** influence **Christianity**?

   _____

   _____

   _____

   _____

4) Briefly explain how **Napoleon** (1769-1821), the **Creoles**, the **Peninsulars**, **King Pedro I** (1798-1834), and the institution of **slavery** were interconnected. _(Be sure to include who sided with whom)._

   _____

   _____

   _____

   _____

   _____

5) Analyze how **Latin America's independence movements** began.

   _____

   _____

6) Who was Jesuit priest **Padre Miguel Hidalgo** (1753-1811) and what role did he play in the massive **peasant** uprising in **Latin America**?

_____

_____

_____

7) Why did the **Creole** General **Agustín Iturbide** (1783-1823) and the **mestizo** commander **Vicente Guerrero** join forces against the **Peninsulars**?

_____

_____

8) Who was **Simon Bolivar** "The Liberator" (1783-1830) and what did he do to further the independence of **Venezuela**?

_____

_____

_____

_____

9) Briefly explain the significance of the outcome in the **Battle of Ayacucho of 1824**.

_____

_____

_____

10) Identify and analyze how **Latin American** independence movements enshrined the idea of **popular sovereignty**.

_____

_____

_____

_____

_____

_____

11) Analyze why countries in **Latin America** that fought for freedom weren't able to keep that freedom even after achieving **independence** during the 19th and 20th centuries.

_____

_____

_____

_____

_____

Coal, Steam, and The Industrial Revolution: Crash Course World History #32

1) Reveal what the world was like before the **Industrial Revolution** (1760-1840).

_____
_____
_____
_____
_____
_____

2) Briefly show how the **Industrial Revolution** (1760-1840) was actually a transition to a new **manufacturing** processes which soon led to an **increase** in **production**.

_____
_____
_____
_____
_____

3) Explain how the **innovations** and **inventions** of the **Industrial Revolution** (1760-1840) are interconnected.

_____
_____
_____
_____
_____
_____
_____
_____

4) Make sense of the multiple arguments and factors surrounding why the **Industrial Revolution** (1760-1840) led to vast social and economic changes in **Great Britain** during the 18th and 19th centuries.

_____
_____
_____
_____
_____

5) How did the **invention** of the **steam engine** change the world over time?

_____
_____
_____
_____
_____
_____
_____
_____

6) Examine and evaluate the advantages **coal** gave to **Europe** (specifically **Great Britain**) in **industrial production** over **China** and **India**.

_____

_____

_____

_____

7) Explain how the **steam engine** was intertwined with the mining of **cheap coal** and furthered the success of the **Industrial Revolution** (1760-1840) in **Great Britain**.

_____

_____

_____

_____

8) Analyze the reasons why **Great Britain** had the highest **wages** in the world around the dawn of the 18th century.

_____

_____

_____

_____

9) Show what **high wages** coupled with **cheap fuel** costs meant for the rise of machines to power the **Industrial Revolution** (1760-1840) in **Great Britain**.

_____

_____

_____

_____

10) Identify how **laborers** in **India** were productive in **textiles** even though they were paid some of the **lowest wages** in the world.

_____

_____

_____

11) Show how **Indian cotton** helped to spark **British industrialization**.

_____

_____

_____

_____

_____

Capitalism and Socialism: Crash Course World History #33

1) Briefly outline the **characteristics** of the **cultural** and **economic system** known as **capitalism**.

_____
_____
_____
_____

2) Explain how people used the **theory** of **mercantile capitalism** to create **joint stock companies,** and go on to explain how this type of **capitalism** works in practice.

_____
_____
_____
_____
_____

3) Point out how **industrial capitalism** is different than **mercantile capitalism** in both in scale and in practice.

_____
_____
_____
_____

4) Identify some of the **negative aspects** of the **economic** and **cultural system** known as **capitalism**.

_____
_____
_____
_____

5) Analyze and evaluate the **origins** of **industrial capitalism** in **Great Britain**.

_____
_____
_____
_____

6) Rationalize how the idea of creating a **positive feedback loop** with **lower food prices** have led to a **richer society** in **England** during the 16th century.

_____
_____
_____
_____
_____

7) Explain how the **British** idea of **enclosure** ultimately lead to an increase of **agricultural productivity** during the 16th century.

_____
_____
_____
_____

8) Show how **capitalism** is also a **cultural system**.

_____
_____
_____
_____

9) Outline the horrors of **capitalism** paying close attention to the **manufacturing sector** and its practices inside of **factories** during the 19th century.

_____
_____
_____
_____

10) Summarize the **political** and **economic theory** of **social organization** known as **socialism**.

_____
_____
_____
_____

11) How did the idea of **class struggle** come to define the **socialist ideas** presented inside of the **Communist Manifesto** (1847) written by author **Karl Marx (1818-1883)**?

_____
_____
_____

12) Outline the **opposing theories** of **class struggle** between the **workers** and the **capitalists**.

_____
_____
_____
_____
_____

13) Identify why **Karl Marx (1818-1883)** and his idea of **socialism** still matters even though the **economic theory of capitalism** seems to have won out in the 21st century.

_____
_____
_____
_____

Samurai, Daimyo, Matthew Perry, and Nationalism: Crash Course World History #34

1) Identify the global phenomenon of how a country's **national awakening** adds to its spread of **nationalism**.

_____
_____
_____
_____

2) Outline the type of **nationalism** that represents the worst aspects of **nationalism**.

_____
_____
_____
_____
_____
_____

3) Define the modern **nation-state** by outlining the differences between a **nation** and a **state**.

_____
_____
_____
_____
_____
_____

4) Identify the differences in arguments between how one becomes part of a **nation** by demonstrating the **cultural** and **ethnic differences** of the state in question.

_____
_____
_____
_____
_____
_____

5) Elaborate on the actual **business** of **nationalization**.

_____
_____
_____
_____
_____
_____

6) Explain how **wars** help to further **national identity**. *(Include examples)*

_____
_____
_____
_____
_____
_____

7) Outline a quick history of the **Tokugawa bakufu** (period of the **Tokugawa shogunate samurai** rule) which ruled **Japan** during the 17th through the 19th centuries.

_____
_____
_____
_____

8) Why do some people such as **Andrew Gordon** in his book, **A Modern History of Japan** (2013), believe that **urban samurai** were a rough and tumble lot?

_____
_____
_____

9) Show how the **Tokugawa Shogunate**, aka **Tokugawa Bakufu,** had difficulty controlling the **great lords,** aka **daimyo**. (*aka means also known as)

_____
_____
_____
_____

10) Explain the repercussions of the **Opium Wars** (1839-1860) on **Japan.**

_____
_____
_____
_____

11) Who was **Matthew Perry** and why did the **Japanese** sign **trade treaties** with him?

_____
_____
_____

12) Explain how **nationalism** was implemented in the **modernization** of **Japan.**

_____
_____
_____
_____
_____
_____
_____
_____

Imperialism: Crash Course World History #35

1) Why did the **Europeans** trade **silver** with **China**?

_____
_____
_____
_____

2) How did the **British Free Trade** policy of the 1830s threaten **China's** favorable balance of trade?

_____
_____
_____
_____
_____

3) Point out the repercussions of **Chinese General Yijing's** (1793-1853) **counterattack** in 1841 upon the **British Royal Navy**.

_____
_____
_____
_____
_____

4) How did the **trade deficit** between **Great Britain** and **China** favor the **Chinese** until after the massive civil war known as the **Taiping Rebellion** (1850-1864)?

_____
_____
_____
_____
_____

5) How did **industrialization** and **nationalism** play a role in the **European colonization** of **Africa**?

_____
_____
_____
_____
_____
_____
_____

6) Analyze the effects that **diseases** such **malaria**, **yellow fever**, and **sleeping sickness** had on **Europeans** (and their horses) while **colonizing Africa**.

_____
_____
_____

_____

_____

_____

7) Analyze and report upon the effects that new **technology** such as **steamships** had on the **British colonization** of **Africa**.

_____

_____

_____

_____

_____

_____

8) Evaluate the reasons why **Europe** came to dominate **Africa**.

_____

_____

_____

_____

_____

_____

9) How did the **British Empire's indirect rule** by **intermediaries** help it to rule **colonies** such as **India**?

_____

_____

_____

_____

_____

10) Why did **native princes** put up with **European imperialism**?

_____

_____

_____

_____

_____

11) Give examples of how some countries resisted **European imperialism**.

_____

_____

_____

_____

_____

_____

Archdukes, Cynicism, and World War 1: Crash Course World History #36

1) How did the **assassination** of **Austrian Archduke Franz Ferdinand** (1863-1914) by **Bosnian Serb Nationalist Gavrilo Princip** (1894-1918) light the powder keg of **World War I** (1914-1919)?

_____
_____
_____
_____
_____
_____
_____

2) Calculate how **Germany**'s inflexible war plan, the **Schlieffen Plan**, only further exacerbated the onset of **World War I** (1914-1919).

_____
_____
_____
_____

3) Compare and contrast the different reasons for the intricate **alliances** between both the **European, African,** and **Asian** nations which inevitably led to **World War I** (1914-1919).

_____
_____
_____
_____
_____
_____

4) Outline the concept surrounding the **glory of nationalism** and how it pertains to the **nationalist** fervor which gripped the world at the outbreak of **World War I** (1914-1919).

_____
_____
_____
_____
_____

5) Calculate and reflect upon the combined length of all the trenches built along the **Western Front**.

_____
_____
_____
_____
_____

6) Analyze what was going on along the **Eastern Front** of **World War 1** (1914-1919) as the **Germans** were fighting against the **Russians**.

_____

_____
_____
_____

7) Evaluate the destructiveness of **World War I** (1914-1919) in terms of **lives lost**, **infrastructure destroyed**, and **psychological effects** on its participants and victims.

_____
_____
_____
_____
_____

8) Identify and evaluate the **Spanish Flu of 1918** that killed people indiscriminately during **World War I** (1914-1919) and culminated in a **pandemic**.

_____
_____
_____
_____
_____

9) How did the inventions of the **machine gun** (1884) and **barbed wire** (1874) change the face of warfare in **World War I** (1914-1919) and lead to events such as the **Battle of the Somme** in the second half of 1916?

_____
_____
_____
_____

10) Justify the reasons why someone could say that there wasn't really anything heroic or glamorous about fighting in **World War I** (1914-1919).

_____
_____
_____
_____
_____

11) Why did soldiers in **World War I** (1914-1919) keep fighting even though the pay was **minimal** and the **conditions** were horrible?

_____
_____
_____
_____
_____

12) Briefly comment on the **terms** under which **Germany** signed the **Treaty of Versailles of 1919** which, in effect, ended **WWI** (1914-1919).

_____
_____
_____
_____
_____
_____
_____

13) Identify and analyze the two phases of the **Russian Revolution of 1917**, which overthrew the **Romanov dynasty** (1613-1917), and eventually established **Vladimir Lennon** (1870-1924) and his **Bolsheviks** to rule over the **Union of Soviet Socialist Republics (USSR)**.

_____
_____
_____
_____
_____
_____
_____
_____

14) How did the introduction of the **United States Army** in 1917 change the war in favor of the **Allied Powers** even though **Germany** had halted its **two front war** by signing a **peace treaty** with **Russia**?

_____
_____
_____
_____
_____
_____
_____
_____

15) Point out the changes which took place in **Africa** after the end of **World War I** (1914-1919).

_____
_____
_____
_____
_____
_____
_____

Essay Prompt World War I

How did **writers** and **artists** of the **Lost Generation** voice their **cynicism** and overall **apathy** towards life both during and after **World War I (**1914-1919)? *(Examples for further study , inclusion, and evaluation outside the Crash Course video component include pieces by painters **John Singer Sargent, Pablo Picasso, and Salvador Dali** as well as literary works by writers **Gertrude Stein, Virginia Woolf, Erich Remarque,** and **Ernest Hemingway**).*

Communists, Nationalists, and China's Revolutions: Crash Course World History #37

1) Point out how the anti-Western **Boxer Rebellion of 1900** stopped the **Chinese** from adopting **European technology** and a self-strengthening **education system**.

_____

_____

_____

_____

_____

2) Identify the importance of **Chinese revolutionary Sun Yat Sen** (1866-1925) and why his three principals of the people: **nationalism, democracy,** and the **people's livelihood** were so popular.

_____

_____

_____

_____

_____

3) Outline the reasons for the success of the **1911 revolution** in **China** which officially ended the **Qing Dynasty** (1644-1912).

_____

_____

_____

_____

4) Determine how the showdown between the **Communists** and the **Nationalists** during the time of the **Chinese Republic** (1912-1949) led to the rise of **Communist** leader **Mao Zedong** (1893-1976).

_____

_____

_____

_____

_____

5) Analyze how the **Chinese Communists** won over the support of the **peasants**.

_____

_____

_____

_____

6) Examine and report upon **Mao Zedong's** (1893-1976) program of **rectification**.

_____

_____

_____

_____
_____
_____
_____

7) Point out how **Mao Zedong** (1893-1976) and the **People's Republic of China (PRC)** created and maintained their new **socialist** state.

_____
_____
_____
_____
_____
_____
_____
_____
_____

8) Analyze the social, political, and economic repercussions of the outset of the **Korean War** (1950-1953) on the mass campaigns launched by **Mao Zedong's** (1893-1976) **democratic dictatorship**.

_____
_____
_____
_____
_____
_____
_____
_____
_____
_____

9) Estimate and analyze the social, political, and economic repercussions that the **final mass campaign**, aka the **Five Anti Campaign**, accomplished by destroying all **capitalism** in **China**. (*aka means also known as)

_____
_____
_____
_____
_____
_____
_____
_____
_____

10) Explain the tactics of **centralized planning** and **collectivization of agriculture** that **Mao Zedong** (1893-1976) and the **CCP** (Chinese Communist Party) used to turn **China** into an **industrial powerhouse**.

_____
_____

_____
_____
_____
_____
_____
_____
_____
_____
_____
_____
_____

11)Identify the problems and subsequent repercussions after **Mao's** implementation of his **Great Leap Forward** system which aimed to increase **industrial productivity**.

_____
_____
_____
_____
_____
_____
_____
_____
_____
_____

12)Point out the successes and failures of the **Cultural Revolution** in **China**.

_____
_____
_____
_____
_____
_____
_____
_____
_____
_____
_____
_____
_____
_____

World War II: Crash Course World History #38

1) Discuss the discrepancies surrounding the start of **World War II** (1939-1945) with some historians saying it began when **Japan** seized **Manchuria** in the **Asian Theatre** in 1931, and others when **Germany** invaded **Poland** in the **European Theatre** in 1939.

_____
_____
_____
_____
_____
_____

2) Point out the brutality that occurred during the **Rape of Nanking** (1937) as an example of the atrocities that took place during **World War II** (1939-1945) and why this event is still so controversial today.

_____
_____
_____
_____
_____
_____

3) Describe **Adolf Hitler's** (1889-1945) rise to power along with his plan of **German Nationalization** that was largely responsible for much of the **European Theatre** of **World War II** (1939-1945).

_____
_____
_____
_____
_____
_____

4) Explain how new types of **mechanized technology** such as tanks, trucks, planes, and novel **infantry tactics** changed the **nature of combat** on the **battlefields** of **World War II** (1939-1945).

_____
_____
_____
_____
_____
_____

5) In the early years of **World War II** (1939-1945), how effective was the **German Blitzkrieg**?

_____
_____
_____
_____
_____

6) Outline the strengths and weaknesses in **the Battle of Britain** (1940) that pitted **the Royal Air Force** against the **German Luftwaffe** during **World War II** (1939-1945).

_____
_____
_____
_____
_____
_____

7) Give a rough idea of what was going on during the **Desert Campaigns** of the **Europeans** fighting in **Africa** during **World War II** (1939-1945).

_____
_____
_____
_____

8) Summarize why **1941** was such a big year for **World War II** (1939-1945).

_____
_____
_____
_____
_____
_____

9) Analyze and evaluate the decision behind the **German** invasion into the **Eastern Front** of **Russia**.

_____
_____
_____
_____
_____
_____

10) Outline the consequences surrounding the events of **December 7, 1941** when the **Japanese** bombed the American Naval base **Pearl Harbor** in **Hawaii**.

_____
_____
_____
_____
_____
_____
_____
_____

11) Identify the chain of events that was going on in the war between **Japan** and **Southeast Asia** and how **Australia** was involved in the fighting against the **Axis** powers.

_____
_____
_____

12) How did the entry of the **United States** into **World War II** (1939-1945) change the outcome of **World War II**?

_____
_____
_____
_____

13) Calculate how **Joseph Stalin** (1878-1953) of **Russia** turned the war against **Germany** with the strategic defeat of the entire **6th army** of the **German Reich** during the **Winter of 1943** in the **Battle of Stalingrad** (1942-1943).

_____
_____
_____
_____
_____
_____

14) Outline the importance of the success of **Canadians, British**, and **American forces** during the Allied invasion on the beaches of **Normandy** in **Operation Overlord** on **D-Day** _(June 6, 1944)._

_____
_____
_____
_____
_____
_____
_____
_____

15) Analyze the importance of the **Allies** defeat of the **Nazis** at the **Battle of the Bulge** in 1944.

_____
_____
_____
_____

16) Briefly mention what happened to **Italy's Benito Mussolini** (1883-1945) and the **German Reich's Adolf Hitler** (1889-1945) in 1945. _(For added knowledge research what happened to **Japan's Hideki Tojo** (1884-1948) in 1948)._

_____
_____
_____

17) How did **Adolf Hitler's** (1889-1945) idea of **Lebensraum** factor into **Germany's** desire to expand its borders?

18) Judge the measure of atrocities committed by the **Nazis** in not only the **concentration** and **labor camps**, but also in the death camps meant to exterminate the **Jews**, **Roma people**, **Communists**, and **homosexuals**.

19) Point out how **Japan's** fear of a **food shortage** was a factor for their resettling of **farmers** in **Korea**.

20) Calculate the deaths around the world by nation due to **World War II** (1939-1945).

21) Show how elements of **Western industrial progress** were warped to slaughter millions in the **Holocaust** during **World War II (**1939-1945**)**.

USA and USSR Fight!: Crash Course World History #39

1) Analyze the clash that occurred between the **economic ideas** of **capitalism** in the **United States of America (USA)**, and **socialism** in the **Union of Soviet Socialist Republics (USSR)** during the **Cold War** (1945-1990).

_____
_____
_____
_____
_____
_____

2) Point out how **nuclear destruction** was now the biggest problem during this **clash of civilizations** for the future of the human race during the **Cold War** (1945-1990).

_____
_____
_____
_____
_____

3) Rationalize why some historians point to the origins of the **Cold War** (1945-1990) as beginning before 1945.

_____
_____
_____
_____
_____
_____

4) Designate how and why **Germany**, along the erection of the **Berlin Wall in 1961**, could be considered as the first battle ground during the **Cold War** (1945-1990).

_____
_____
_____
_____
_____
_____
_____

5) Outline the general idea understood inside of the **United States Policy of Containment** that was used in order to stop the spread of **Communism**.

_____
_____
_____
_____
_____
_____

6) Go into detail on the **Marshall Plan** and include how that plan would **rebuild Europe** after **World War II** (1939-1945) and **stop** the spread of **Communism**.

_____

_____

_____

_____

7) Explain what was going on during the **nuclear arms race** during the second half of the **20th century**.

_____

_____

_____

_____

_____

_____

_____

_____

8) Identify how the **Western** belief in the **domino effect** led to the **Korean War** (1950-1953) and the **Vietnam War** (1955-1975) during the **Cold War** (1945-1990).

_____

_____

_____

_____

_____

_____

9) Point out the expansion of the **Cold War** (1945-1990) between the **USA** and **USSR** into other places of the world.

_____

_____

_____

_____

_____

_____

_____

_____

10) Explain how the planet was divided into three different worlds during the **Cold War** (1945-1990)

a) _____

_____

_____

b) _____
_____
_____

c) _____
_____
_____

11) Why wasn't the idea of a world built upon **capitalism** an easy choice for **third world countries** caught up in the middle of the **Cold War** (1945-1990) battle between the **USA** and the **USSR**?

_____
_____
_____
_____
_____
_____
_____
_____
_____

12) Why didn't **Soviet Socialism** prove to be a viable alternative to **industrial capitalism**?

_____
_____
_____
_____
_____
_____
_____
_____
_____

13) How did the **Russian ideas** of **Glasnost** and **Perestroika** help to end the **Cold War** (1945-1990)

_____
_____
_____
_____
_____
_____
_____
_____
_____
_____
_____

Decolonization and Nationalism Triumphant: Crash Course World History #40

1) How did **World War II** (1939-1945) keep **colonial empires** from expanding and ultimately discredit the whole idea of creating **empires**?

_____
_____
_____
_____

2) Explain how the big **colonial** powers of **France, Britain**, and **Japan** were significantly weakened by **World War II** (1939-1945).

_____
_____
_____
_____
_____
_____

3) In a nutshell, explain the characteristics of **decolonization.**

_____
_____
_____
_____
_____
_____

4) Explain how **Mahatma Gandhi**'s (1869-1948) leadership of mass **non-violent protests** and **hunger strikes** led to **decolonization** in **India.**

_____
_____
_____
_____
_____
_____
_____

5) Explain the reality of what happened to **India** when **India** gained its independence from **Britain**.

_____
_____
_____
_____
_____

6) Show how the **Japanese** furthered the cause of **Indonesian nationalism** even though **Indonesia** was a **Dutch colony**.

_____
_____
_____
_____

7) Show how the end of **colonization** and the rule of **Cambodian communists Khmer Rouge** with its leader **Pol Pot** (1925-1998) was disastrous in **Cambodia**.

_____

_____

_____

_____

8) Show how the **communists** in **Vietnam,** under the leadership of **Ho Chi Minh** from 1945-1969, eventually separated themselves from first **French colonial** rule and then **American colonial** rule.

_____

_____

_____

_____

9) What problems did **Egyptian army** commander **Gamal Abdel Nasser** (1918-1970), and ruler of **Egypt** from 1956-1970, create after gaining complete control of **Egypt**.

_____

_____

_____

_____

10) Compare and contrast what **European nations** claimed to do for countries in **Africa** in comparison to what **European nations** actually did.

_____

_____

_____

_____

_____

11) Identify a few military leaders who exploited the **postwar industrial world** and took control various countries of Africa.

_____

_____

_____

_____

12) Outline a few countries in **Africa** that had success during the **postwar industrial world**.

_____

_____

_____

_____

Globalization I: Crash Course World History #41

1) How does your t-shirt tell the story of **globalization**?

_____
_____
_____
_____

2) How has trade increased today since the early **Indus Valley Civilization** that traded goods thousands of years ago?
A)_____
B)_____
C)_____

3) Which country makes most of our t-shirts and why?

_____
_____
_____

4) Explain how **South America, the Caribbean, and Africa** have been "bullied" into trading with larger **economies** around the world.

_____
_____
_____

5) Explain the **Industrial Revolution** which occurred around the world in the 19th century.

_____
_____
_____

6) How has **global capitalism** been good for a lot of people?

_____
_____
_____
_____
_____

7) Briefly point out how more than 6 million people been lifted out of **poverty** due to **globalization**.

_____
_____
_____
_____

8) Name some of the **side-effects** of **globalization**.

_____
_____
_____
_____

9) Give three reasons why has **migration** become easier due to **globalization**.

A)_____
_____

B)_____
_____

C)_____
_____

10) Give some examples and the effects of a **globalized culture**.

_____
_____
_____
_____

11) How has **globalization** changed us for the better?

_____
_____
_____
_____

12) Why do modern humans live twice as long as people who lived just a **century** ago?

_____
_____
_____
_____
_____

13) Rationalize the reasons why people study history.

_____
_____
_____
_____
_____
_____
_____

14) Why do modern humans feel invincible and powerful now?

_____
_____
_____
_____
_____

Globalization II - Good or Bad?: Crash Course World History #42

1) Explain how the **psychology** of living in the **21st century** inside of the upper classes of the **industrial world** shapes our human **reality** and existence. *(Hint: Think about and describe the meal you last ate and how it got to your table.)*

_____

_____

_____

_____

_____

2) Analyze how **globalization** has led to a celebration of **individualism**.

_____

_____

_____

3) Point out the harsh realities and the **limitations of freedom** experienced by the generation of human beings who lived through the **Great Depression** (1929-1939) and **World War II** (1939-1945).

_____

_____

_____

_____

_____

4) Judge how the availability of **contraception** has changed and reshaped the nature of **reproduction** between individuals of the **human species**.

_____

_____

_____

_____

_____

5) Identify the biggest repercussion of **globalization** and how the rise in the **human population** has affected the **environment**.

_____

_____

_____

_____

_____

6) Determine the effects of how the **increase of consumption** and **worldwide production** has strained **natural resources**.

_____

_____

_____

_____
_____
_____
_____

7) Outline the **virtuous cycle** of growth inside of the **Industrial Revolution** (1760-1840) and what that has done to the earth.

_____
_____
_____
_____
_____
_____
_____
_____
_____
_____
_____
_____

8) Demonstrate why it is strange that there haven't been more **pandemics**, such as the **Spanish Flu of 1918** in the 20th and 21st centuries, even though the **population** has **increased**.

_____
_____
_____
_____
_____
_____
_____
_____

9) Rationalize how some people argue that an **economically interdependent** world is less likely to go to war then an **economically independent** world. *(Hint: Think of where your shirt came from and how it was made and by whom).*

_____
_____
_____
_____
_____
_____
_____
_____

10) Show how **South Africa** has changed from an **Apartheid** to a **Democracy**.

_____
_____
_____
_____
_____
_____

11) Evaluate how the **rise of globalization** could be dangerous to the **human race**.

12) Take into account the **technological devices** that shape your existence today and then imagine how **continuing globalization** coupled with **new technological innovations** will shape the future.

_____
_____
_____
_____
_____
_____
_____
_____
_____
_____
_____
_____
_____
_____
_____
_____
_____
_____
_____
_____
_____
_____
_____
_____
_____
_____
_____
_____
_____
_____
_____
_____
_____
_____
_____
_____

Notes